PHYSICS
ON ALL FOURS

To Bettina—

with much love

Nick

♡ ♡♡

2/8/01

Illustrations by Khola Herbert

Some poems have previously appeared in:
MONDO 2000, Berkeley
Future Sex, San Francisco
Island Views, Santa Cruz
Moorish Science Monitor, Tucson
EGO 2000, Amsterdam
and in the cruzio e-zines
Hawk
Zero City

I am grateful to the editors
of these fine publications
and to the owners and clientele of
BOULDER CREEK BISTRO
where many of these works
were first performed.

Sea Creature Press
Box 261
Boulder Creek, CA 95006

PHYSICS
ON ALL FOURS
NICK HERBERT
SELECTED VERSE 1995-2000

Sea Creature Press
Boulder Creek, CA
2000

PREFACE: PHYSICS ON ALL FOURS

Every Big Idea starts small: as tentative, half-formed, embryonic notions. Every revolution begins with vague complaints. Every king was once a tot. Launching a new science is no different.

I call it Quantum Tantra--the Science of the New Millennium. In his long Latin poem **De Rerum Natura** Lucretius publicized the (materialist) science of his day. Likewise in my verse I scatter the seeds of tomorrow's brand-new (immaterialist) physics.

Quantum Tantra aims to contact Nature directly, not by external observation as our present physics does so well, but by joining our inner lives to the inner lives of what we now regard as objects. "In all forms of things there is a Mind," William Wordsworth proposed. The goal of Quantum Tantra is to touch the minds in things using empathy-amplifying tools derived from quantum physics. See "Jabir's Formula" on page 41 for QT's most concise formulation.

I've divided this book into four parts, the first a meandering meditation on what might be considered "religious" topics, including contact with aliens (who QT supposes more reachable mind-to-mind rather than via metal ships.)

Part Two focuses on Quantum Tantra itself--first baby steps into interior relativity (with all beings we shall be as relatives) flowing from a physics unafraid to open itself to Nature's deepest embraces. I am courting a new sensual science here--my foreplay: these few clumsy verses.

Part Three briefly considers what Green Man Dale Pendall calls "The Poison Path"--the careful use of mind-altering plants to explore Self & Nature from the inside--a crude foretaste of the day when not chemistry but physics shapes dependable passkeys for "unlocking the doors of perception".

Part Four returning to more traditional themes ("But the sea is awash with roses"--Patchen) climaxes with Elements of Tantra--the unofficial anthem of the New Millennial Science.

As befits an immature enterprise, these verses are simple, bold, playful and sometimes impertinent. For opening numerous doors, I thank my ineffable Muse and Her many lovely helpers.

Nick Herbert
Boulder Creek, California
quanta@cruzio.com
http://members.cruzio.com/~quanta
http://quantumtantra.com

TABLE OF CONTENTS

SLOVAK SCIENCE
(for Mom and Dad)

My mother was Slovakian
My father from the Ukraine
Our name "Gorbesh" mangled
To "Herbert" at Ellis Island
By some assholes with badges
Who spoke nothing but English.

You call yourselves the Master Race?
The Chosen People?
The Beloved of Allah?
Then kill me now
For I despise all your tribes equally
And place my allegiance elsewhere.
Tribalism is the deadly schoolyard game
Played now by apes with Plutonium:
My team is bigger, better, smarter
My Dad can beat up yours.

He call me
NiggerNaziSlovakJew
I twist off his testicles
I murder all his babies.

I say any woman
With a baby at her breast
Is more manly
Than any of you tribalists.

1

NiggerNaziSlovakJew
We are all Chosen People
Or we are all doomed.
Ask any man or woman
who is raising a child:
Each of us is Chosen at birth
We are all Chosen People
Or we are all doomed.

We were three Slovak households
In a neighborhood full of wops.
There were plenty of reasons to fight
And finding none
We'd make one up.

I am no better than any of you
I remember making a fist of my hand
And striking another's face
In righteous anger.
I KNOW HOW GOOD IT FEELS
To connect, with knuckles
To punish, with blows
To show the woman who's boss.

Every tribe has its truths
It will kill to keep from knowing
Science is a fragile flame
Truth-seeking a dangerous calling
Even the best of tribes
Will turn savage
And hunt down its finest scientists
Like dogs.

So when Jack calls me "stooge" or worse
I cring
Not for myself
But for the sake of science
Feeling the lure of that easy slide
Into barbarism.

I am no better than any of you
NiggerNaziSlovakJew
For I too am in love with that swamp
That low way flows in my blood and body
That low way feels hale and normal to me.

But at my best
I yearn to move to deeper rhythms
Streaming up from dark reality's core
Daily I practice not to flee the forbidden
Not to shun the outcast, the part that doesn't fit.

For what is the way of science if not this:
This continual casting out of fear?

I am not afraid of you
I want to listen closely
To All of Your Stories
NiggerNaziSlovakJew
Please speak freely
From your heart to mine.

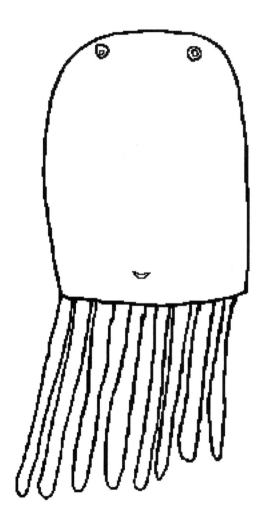

YELLOW COTTON PRAYER FLAGS

MAYA

I knew all the time that your offer was phony
But I went along just for laughs
I knew all along that you planned to kill me
but I played along because it was warm
I played along because it tasted sweet
I played along
          because it reminded me of someplace else

I knew all the time that it was an illusion
But I went along because I liked the smell of it
I played along because I liked the taste of it
I played along because I liked the way it felt
                              especially under water

Even tho I knew it was an illusion
Even tho I knew it was a dream
I liked the way it moved
I liked the sounds it made
I liked the way it all fit together
I liked the way it pulsated at my touch
I liked the way it gave off light
                    especially after dark.

Even tho I knew it was an illusion
I loved it all
Loved every apparent pleasure
Loved the way it seemed to hurt
Loved all the lies, the tricks, the make-believe

Loved the stage sets, the makeup, the tacky props
Loved every unreal second
Loved every male mannikin
Loved every female impersonator
Loved every fraudulent molecule
Loved every phony atom
I was completely fooled
I was entirely taken in.

I loved it all
I really fell for it.

MAGDALENA I
(For Theodora)

What Christian would not somersault with glee
To travel back to ancient Galilee?
To walk barefoot on Israel's holy ground
And videotape the Sermon on the Mound?

Then envy me, for I lived in His time
I knew the Man: we shared a glass of wine
And later on this not unpleasing bod
Was wrapped around the very limb of God.

What Christian would not sell his wife and farm
To listen to His voice or touch His arm?
I walked and touched and harkened to His word
And felt His first and second coming, and His third.

I held Him heard Him sobbing in His sleep
He dreamt of nails punching thru His feet
To me alone He spoke His Secret Name
And which of you could ever say the same?

MAGDALENA II

After the handshake
We uncorked the wine and talked
Then he used his lips on me
Like nobody before or since
He was shy and afraid
But this man knew exactly
How a woman is put together.

After I came
He caressed my hair
As I mouthed his sacks
As I took the root between my lips.

I explored him orally
Till the candles died
Then sometime in the dark
He held my head and moaned
And I swallowed his seed:
  Seed of Solomon and David
  Seed of Abraham and Melchizedek.

I was nineteen then
As young as my grand-daughter Sophia
But I still remember
How it tasted:
Bitter
Like seasalts and myrrh.

Just another blowjob?
I think not.
That man was divine.

NO KNOWLEDGE

John Locke
George Berkeley
David Hume:
No knowledge is possible
Unless it come thru the senses.

Thru the window by the computer
Odor of night-blooming jasmine
Outdoors, moon and candlelight
Mingle with my bath water.

Beyond words
Beyond number
Outside of space and time
I diligently seek a glimpse
Of Her sweet wisdom mind.

What's Sophia's lesson tonight
Under the warm September moon?
That countless are the men
Who knew satori, nirvana
                 nirvikalpa samadhi
                 as She milked the seed
                 from their testicles.

MONTEREY BAY CYCLE SLUT

She responds to the pull of the moon
Twice a day
The Eastward-turning Earth
Drags her tidal bulge cross this beach
Gainst lunar gravity's distant tug.

She responds to the pull of the moon
Her waters teem with microscopic life styles
Her waves brim with sticky fishes
       with wet diatoms
       with invisible sperm and egg
       with metric tons of slick crustaceans.
All night her depths glisten with signals
Human-unreadable mood exchange
Between billions of luminescent mind.

She responds to the pull of the moon
She travels round the world with gangs of men
She flaunts her body, howls, eats strange drugs
She is uncontrollable
She murders her children
She nurses her young on her breasts
She is every sailor's wet dream
She feeds the hungry, heals the sick, buries the dead
She leaves blood on the sheets
She copulates on all fours
She will never stop weeping.

BUDDHA NATURE

Two metaphors for
Ashley Walker (1954-1995)

Yellow cotton prayer flags
flying over Vajrapani:
standing for
this life's lovely emptiness.

Purple cotton panties
drying on your clothesline:
standing for
this world's empty loveliness.

SACRED SPACES

Stonehenge, New Grange
Crop circles, Glastonbury Tor
My sacred sites are Her eyes
Her nipples, the whorls on Her fingertips--
Are the origins and insertions of Her muscles
Are the places where Her bones meet
Are the follicles of Her hair
Are the pads of Her feet, Her buttocks, the slots
Between Her toes.

NINETY-NINE NAMES OF GODDESS

She is the Beginning and the End
She is Galaxy and Garden
She is the Sun and the Moon
She is Atom and the Void
She is Wisdom personified:
She is Sophia

She is Annie, Allegra, Allison, Athena and Alex
She is Beverly, Betsy, Bobbie, Bella and Beth

She is the Earth and the Sea
She is Fire and Ice
She is Energy and Time
She is Root and Bloom
She is Beauty embodied:
She is Aphrodite

She is Carla, Carol, Cindy, Christine and Kate
She is Donna, Diana, Denby, Dorcas and Dannie

She is Pain and Pleasure
She is Bear, Butterfly, Octopus and Eel
She is Prairie Grass and Marijuana
She is Sound and Sight
She is Smell, Taste and Touch
She is Life on the loose:
She is Daphne

She is Marilyn, Margie, Marsha, Mary, Marie, Magdalena
She is Laura, Louise, Liane, Lena, Lise and Lorraine

She is Darkness and Light
She is Consciousness and Slumber
She is Silver and Gold
She is Magnesium, Tungsten, Lithium, Lead
She is Carbon, Argon, Niobium and Starlight
She is the Space Between the Stars
She is the Angel of Death:
She is Kali

She is Sheila, Sherry, Sharma, Stephanie, Stella & Sarah
She is Salima, Shelly, Suzie, Lila, Cici and Mollie
She is Andra, Patty, Elaine, Elizabeth, Karen, Philippa
She is Debbie, Isabel, Ida, Nancy, Janice, JoAnn

She is Unnameable, Unspeakable
She is Terror and Bliss
She is Nourishment and Intoxication
She is the Ocean and the Source
She is the Mother of Animals
She is the Juice in Things:
She is Shakti

She is Illusion and Reality
White and Black
Male and Female
Birth and Death
She is the Wild Muse that inspires us
She is the Mystery that surrounds us
She is Everything and Nothingness
She is the Beginning and the End.

FIRST CONTACT

To open ourselves to pleasure:
It's what the aliens want to teach us
For who would wish telepathic union
                   with a world of whiners?

Aliens call Earth
"Planet of the Hates"
We are so bitter, so backwards
so cruel and filled with pain.

All acts of love and pleasure
Are invitations to alien contact.
Are you ready to merge
               with the Neighboring Other?
Have you freed yourself from hatred?
Have you made your mind
                 a splendid pleasure dome?
Have you adorned yourself as a bridegroom?
Have you adorned yourself as a temple prostitute
offering your golden body at bargain rate?

Are you ready to merge
               with the Neighboring Other?
Have you made your mind a worthy playground
for beings with superior notions of play?
What substances have you ingested
to make your mind receptive
to unearthly forms of enjoyment?

Are you prepared to surrender your body fully
to alien pleasure transmissions?
Are you prepared to surrender your mind fully
tTo an otherworldly Physics of Orgasm?

Yes, they all want to marry our sisters.
Yes, and want us all to marry THEIR SISTERS too.

All acts of love and pleasure
Are invitations to alien contact.
Are you ready to join the Galactic Club?
They are opening their warm arms
Their sticky tentacles, their moist fur-lined cavities
to Earth's uniquely beautiful males and females.

They know what they want--they made the first move
They have touched us gently so as not to frighten.
They are open and yearning for contact.
What then holds you back
from joining the Galactic Dance?
What then holds you back
from wholeheartedly embracing
                    the beckoning Cosmos?

ALIENS ANNOUNCE
IMMINENT HUMAN UPGRADE!
HOMO SAPIENS 1.5

Physicist, heal thyself
Submit to Alien Pleasure Rays
Before We let you board a starship
We'd like to teach humanity to play
We'd love to show you yesterday
                    when yesterday was called "today".

But first
We'll need to wean you from your "X-and-Y"s and "pi"s
And feed you ribs, and naked breasts and tender thighs
Before We help humanity to fly
We'd like to see how passionate you cry
We'll even teach you how to nicely die.

Before We let you in the Pan-Galactic Club
We'll show you how attentively to rub
Rub shoulders, haunches, crotches, tendrils, feet
Of lovely mindful lifeforms
                    in quantum wave-entangled heaps
Of expressive hairy strangers
                    with the strangest sexual needs
That too much astral travelling at extra-light-fast speeds
Can bring about.

Don't ask Us: how much, how many and what for?
Make love just once with Us then open up for more
Before We open up for you that well-kept Secret Door

To Nature and the Bigger Tribes next door
To hypersexual pan-galactic corridors
To alien wolf packs, fairy kingdoms,

                           outlaw gangs galore
And all the million billion secrets of amor.

Please open up, amigos, unclench yourselves,

                               invite Us in
We'll show you fifteen hundred different types of sin
And fifty million kinds of lovely pleasuring
From deep red-shifted clusters, spiral nebula

                            beyond the Rim
From love-starved quantum creatures

                  neither It nor They nor She & Him
Accept Our Gifts
Of pleasure tools, telepathy, Empath Juice and

                          Wisdom Weed
Of bulbous bulging sacks of alien eggs and seeds
And six new senses that your species really needs

                          for time travel.

Open up for Me: I sense you'll really like it.
Open up for Me: I feel you'll really like it.
Open up for Me: I know you'll really like it.

Come live with Me and be My Love
And we will all the pleasures prove
So we may all the pleasures prove
Come live with Me and be My Love.

REVOLUTION

Our starry galaxy turns on its axis
Milky Way stirring like cream
In the coffee-black darkness of night
And the Sun turns too
Likewise the Earth & the Moon.

A man and a woman at Radio Beach
Holding hands leaning backwards
Spinning barefoot on the sand.

Every photon is spinning
Every quark and electron too.
From their spinning comes magnetism
From their spinning comes the Order of the Elerments
And the bonds that hold our bodies together.

Evey photon is spinning
Every quark and electron too:
It is that kind of Universe.

Imitating the Universe the dervish spins too
Bare feet bare feet bare feet on the hardwood floor.
"I am dizzy," he cries.

I am dizzy
I am dizzy
I am dizzy
With love for You.

TANTRIC CATECHISM
(To adore anything less than All of Her
is to worship a fetish--Doctor Jabir)

Why is this tubed cosmetic holy?
Because she has touched it
With the lips of her mouth.

Why is this dark brown earth holy?
Because she has touched it
With the soles of her feet.

Why is this elusive air holy?
Because she has touched it
With the alveoli of her lungs.

Why is this flowing water holy?
Because of many times passing thru her body
Touching her flesh from inside.

Why is this kindled fire holy?
Because she too warms this space
With her biological fire.

Why is this common garment holy?
Because she has kissed it repeatedly
With the lips of her vulva.

DEATH ANGEL

When I meet the angel of death
Will She be lovely and voluptuous?
When She catch my wary eye
Will I see in Her face
        all that I have ever loved
        reflected back as in a magic mirror?

When I meet the angel of death
Will She be lovely and voluptuous?
When She take my hand in Hers
Will it feel like stumbling backwards
                into a piece of music?
Will death be like falling back into dreamless sleep?
Will death be like dissolving back into the elements?
        back into Carbon, Nitrogen &
                Phosphorus?
        back into the Earth?
        back into the Air?
        back into the Water, the Fire?
        back into the luminiferous Ether?
Will dying resemble collapsing into Black Vacuum?
Will dying remind me of falling in love?

When I meet the angel of death
Will She be lovely and voluptuous?
When She kiss me with Her promiscuous mouth
Will Her kisses drive me out of this world?
            out of this body?
            out of this mind?

When I meet the angel of death
Will She be lovely and voluptuous?
When She take me in Her ancient arms
Will Her beauty take my breath away?
Will Her beauty make me blind, make me deaf?

When I meet the angel of death
Will She be lovely and voluptuous?
When She strip the clothes from my body
Will Her eagerness make me out of breath?
                              out of sight?
                              out of hearing?
                              out of here?

When I meet the angel of death
Will She be lovely and voluptuous?
When She press Her irresistable body to mine
How will Her angelic skin feel to my touch?
What will death smell like?
How will She taste?

When I meet the angel of death
Will She be lovely and voluptuous?
Will She be That One Woman
I have been seeking all my life
In the arms of others?

When I meet the angel of death
Will She be lovely and voluptuous?
Will She be That One Woman
I have been dying to meet?

I WANT TO WOO HER
NOT VIEW HER

META-DOCTORS ON DUTY

Doctor Jabir's the metaphysician
For those deep philosophical pains
For those troubles we've all had since Eden
For those problems burnt into our brains.

Who am I? And what are you?
And is One and One makes Two
A made-up noise or universal?
Is this mad drama dream or real
                    or simply a rehearsal?

Is there a God or is She not?
Should I believe what I've been taught?
Or should I go it all alone?
Can one find wisdom on one's own?

Cosmetic repair
On this kettle of flesh?
Where meat doctor staggers
Met-doctor's still fresh.

Is it One or is it Many?
Is it moving? Is it still?
Is it conscious? Is it sleeping?
What happens when I take this pill?

Some suffer from a bone-deep fear
That matter's all that matters here
That love and hate and pretty faces
Are naught but atoms changing places.

For constipated ideology
Say, science as idolatry
We meta-doctors recommend
LSD enemas--at least ten.

From Leningrad to Olduvai
We all suffer: we all cry:
"Doctor, Doctor, will I die?
Tell me truth and do not lie."

Brother, Sister, take my word
From everything I've seen and heard
While practicing philosophy
I swear upon my PhD
You'll get no truer Truth from me.

Don't worry; don't wonder
Don't doubt this:
Death has your number
She won't miss
So give your life one final kiss
The surest truth in medicine
Is that we doctors never win.

The most powerful drug
In Jabir's meta-kit
Is Absolute Certitude
You will be hit.

Life's first lesson is death
And now that you know
Will death get you down, or
Make every sense glow?

QUANTUM REALITY

"Physicists no longer conceptualize matter
as the force-driven motion of independent objects
but rather as the chancy interplay of contextual
possibilities."
--Doctor Jabir

Shall I look at Her
Or shall I not?

Hard, small, separated
If I look;
Soft, spread-out, connected
If I don't.

Hard particle and soft wave: both?
Small right-here and spread-out everywhere: both?
Deep connected yet lonely separate?

Honey
Some day You gotta show me
How You do that.

SCHRÖ DINGER CAT NAP

Tonight while you're asleep
I'd like to superpose my body over yours
Schrödinger-Cat style
Aligning our buzzing possibility waves
Till each cell of me's
In closest quantum association
With each cell of thee.

Our hearts aligned, our pulses
Our lungs aligned, our breathings
Our brainwaves, our pelvic twitches
Every capillary's motion
Completely in sync.

I'd like to enter you fully, love
In a way no other man has ever imagined.

For a time with you
I'd like to experience quantum entanglement
Not cold mathematical but warm first-hand
I'd like to feel naked superposition
Then letting my busy mind go
Falling asleep inside you
Going to sleep me added to you and
Co-experience our first two-person dream.

Then waking before you do
Take my leave gently
Breaking our superposition
Unravelling our mutual possibilities
Leave only our phases intermingling
Like tangled bed clothing

Now alone in my bed
I recall what I've read
About the quantum connection:
No space there, no time
So the physicists say
So for billions of years, dear
We've slept together this way.

QUANTUM CONJECTURE
ON THE HARD PROBLEM
OF CONSCIOUSNESS
(For David Chalmers)

Light glistening thru the glassy air
Undulates like waves you float on
Until light strikes some open eye
That turns it into actual photon.

This is the World of the Quantum Mechanic
Not the Butcher nor Baker nor Cook:
It's possibility waves when unregarded
It's actual particles whenever you look.

In utter darkness safe from leerers
Huge Waves of Maybe surged and swam
But when I turned to look at them
They turned to little Bits of Am.

What means "looking"? I don't know.
You'll have to ask Professor Joe
And Joe asks Sue and Sue asks Dick
And he asks Ruth and she asks Nick
Who gives them all a dirty look
And recommends you buy his book.

Though looking any kid can do
Dumb physicists don't have a clue
How using your bare sense of sightness
You wrench real matter out of mightness.

In the land of Only Possible
Every living thing would die
My cat must feast
On actual meat
And so must thee and she and I.

I cite Stapp, my Muse, Saint John and Wigner
We all assume what "looking" means:
That particles emerge from waveness
To satisfy some creature's needs.

At whatever level life awakens
It lurks there feeling waves go by
Consults its belly, reaches out--
Then waves turn into apple pie.

THOUSAND SCIENCE

How can I
Her spread-open Body know
from lovely head
to lowly toe?
I'll kick back
knuckle under
slow down
open up
and
let a thousand science grow
For what can I expect to know
from one, from one
from only one
way of looking at Her?

THE TAO OF PHYSICS

That State you can state is not things-as-they-are
Language, like highway, goes only so far
Unnamed is the Source from which everything springs
Naming gives rise to the "Ten Thousand Things"
Unlooked at: She exceeds what can possibly be
What you get when you look? No more than you see
Yet the world She is One whether looked at or not
Nature's own nature's not something that's taught
But reach out to feel Her invisible flesh
Hear, see and smell: everything fresh!

PHYSICS FOR BEGINNERS

I remove
Her outer coverings
She shows me
the very center of Her Being.

When words falter
I reach for my mathematics
Mostly She eludes description.

I remove
Her inner coverings
She shows me
a deep Nothingness
simpler and more powerful
than all of my Somethingnesses
put together.

I catch Her eye
She smiles
She opens Her Paradox
and takes out Her Mystery.

SEX MANUAL

Love is the best lubricant
Mind the best sex toy
Darkness the best light
Spirit the hottest erogenous zone

Smell is the best sex drug
Eye-play the warmest caress
Touch the best language
Taste the most intimate gesture

Silence the best music
Desire the best teacher
Yes, naked desire is the best teacher
And silence the best music

Taste the most intimate gesture
Touch the best language
Eye-play the warmest caress
Smell the best sex drug

Spirit the hottest erogenous zone
Darkness the best light
Mind is the best sex toy
Love is the best lubricant.

ELEMENTAL MIND

O Lulu, Lila, Lily, Lola
Lillian, Lutetium, Louise
Lanthium, Lithium, Lawrencium, Lead
O laughter, lust and longitude
O lipstick, language, lagoon

O what I first heard and saw
O what I heard and saw next
O what I hear and see this moment
O what I will finally hear and see.

O Lulu, Lila, Lily, Lola
Lillian, Lutetium, Louise
Lanthium, Lithium, Lawrencium, Lead
O lucite, lizard, lodestone, leaf
O lubricant, lupine, long division

O what I first smelled and tasted
O what I smelled and tasted next
O what I smell and taste right now
O what I will finally smell and taste.

O Lulu, Lila, Lily, Lola
Lillian, Lutetium, Louise
Lanthium, Lithium, Lawrencium, Lead
O lightning, lingerie, lollipop, leaf
O lion, Los Alamos and Lourdes

O the first breath I took
O the breaths I took next
O this breath I take now
O my last breath.

O Lulu, Lila, Lily, Lola
Lillian, Lutetium, Louise
Lanthium, Lithium, Lawrencium, Lead
O lavender, lava, Lycra and lace
O natural law; O lawless nature

O first love
O past love
O latest love
O last love

O love at first sight.

MIND REACH

When I push up the barbell, it pushes me back
With an equal force aimed at the floor
The fact that each action compels a reaction
Is what makes rocket ships soar.

When I'm tasting an apple, does it taste me back?
Is conscious intention a two-way caress?
When I kissed your labia in my imagination
Did you feel my mind touching you
                        under your dress?

I've ransacked the legends of quantum physics
Of voodoo and magic shamanic arts
I've experienced the TimeSpace Without Separation
Before we divided Her into Her Parts.

I'd like to boldly touch you
Where no man's touched before
I'd love to be the Ocean
That breaks upon your shore.

I'd love to astrally fuck you
With my fully extended wit
As foreplay for fucking Nature
In every open slit.

JABIR'S FORMULA

I want to woo Her, not view Her
Pet Reality until She purrs
Yearning to merge with Dame Nature bodily
Longing to mingle my substance with Hers:
And them content with merely observing
Are nothing but Nature's voyeurs.

JABIR'S FORMEL

Ich möchte ihr den Hof machen, sie nicht nur betrachten
Realität streicheln bis sie schnurrt
Körperlich mich mit Madame Natur vereinen
Meine Substanz sehnsüchtig mit ihr vermischen:
Und wer befriedigt schon beim beobachten
Ist nicht mehr als ein Voyeur der Natur.

trans. by Max Weiss

THE MAN WHO MARRIED THE SEA

Will you marry me? said the sea
Will you take my name?
Yes I will, I answered back
And to the sea I came.

Will you marry me? said the sea
Would you be my fiancée?
I've spread myself beneath the moon
In kelp and coral lingerie.

Will you marry my estuary?
Will you copulate with my slough?
Do you take my foamy white breakers
I will, said I, and I do.

But would you dare to wed the sea?
We practice deep polygamy
So He, She, It would marry thee
And no one ever leaves the sea.

Will you marry me? said the sea
Would you share my deep salty life?
Would you be the sea's newest husband?
Would you be the ocean's next wife?

Will you marry me? said the sea
Would you offer me your heart?
Why get married? my heart replied
I've belonged to the sea from the Start.

HAPPY DOOMSDAY

Warmest Telepathic Greetings
To all sentient lifeforms!

Every sufficiently advanced culture
Celebrates that day
When they first make contact
With the heartful MindForms
That dwell inside all Matter.
Old tribalists obsessed with hate and swindlehoax
Resist Deep Meeting as a kind of Doomsday--
Catastrophic to their petty dreams of conquest.
For the rest of us it has opened the Universe
To joyous brother-and-sisterly exploration.
May Earth experience this Opening soon:
Humans have lived alone for a very long time.

This was the day we discovered the Door
That is open to all from the Start
This was the day we traded in War
In exchange for a wide-open Heart
This is the birthday of Love and of Life and the Child--
The day when we tore off our diapers
And entangled our lives with the Wild.

FIVE QUANTUM TANTRIC LIMERICKS

The purpose of yin-style Chi Gung
a practice I've barely begun
is to open up holes
whose delicate roles
will surpass the tact of the tongue

To the novice the biggest surprise
is to see without using his eyes
the numerous threads
connecting our heads
and the ribbons entangling our thighs

With new orifices, apertures, holes
new meanings, new purposes, goals
we've opened our hearts
and our new private parts
to an invisible Network of Souls

Thru our tantric antenna array
we find new things to hear and to say
to our lovers in bed
to the recently dead
to our friends from the Deep Milky Way

We fornicate photons in chemical trances
we welcome fresh alien sexual advances
we're big girls and boyses
who've outgrown our toyses
we've extraterrestrially opened **our pantses**.

FASTIDIOUS PHYSICISTS

Nature's hinting there's new ways to meet Her
More intense, more engaging--and sweeter
But like shy maiden aunts
We say "O dear me, no!" to Her Dance
"We'd rather be reading our meters."

FETISH PHYSICS

You physicists are terrified to kiss Dame Nature
In hot entangled polysexual play--
No, you've barely got the balls to sniff
Her cold and dead discarded lingerie.

ALEXA

Physicists say
everything that exists
is made of elemental events
called quanta.

And the occurrence
in space and time
of these world-making events
is utterly random.

For those
to whom physics
means mathematical mastery of nature
the discovery of sheer randomness
at the heart of things
was a hard slap in the face.

And why call it "random"?

Why not "unprecedented"?, "improvisational"?
Why not name it "comes-out-of-nowhere"?
Why not call it "Surprise!"?

I play at calling it "Alexa":
She who is beyond the law.
Alexa is unruly, untamed, illicit
She is one chance in a million, the lucky break
we call Her hitting the jackpot, breaking the bank
we call Her windfall, wildcat, hitting paydirt
tapping the mother lode, striking it rich.

Alexa is willful, disobedient, out of bounds
She is the cut of the cards, the roll of the die,
                              the spin of the wheel
She is Donna Fortuna, sleeping with gamblers
She favors boldness and risktakers
and loads the dice (some say) in their favor.

Alexa moves outside of your logical categories
She breaks fences, agreements,
                              international boundaries
She is pirate treasure, ill-gotten loot, contraband
She is an uncontrolled substance
She is love at first sight.

Alexa created symphonies, foxes and neutron stars
She is the mother of invention
She is mama coyote: she will trick you
She hides the cards up her sleeve
She is Lady Luck.

Alexa is the looseness, the slack, the give in things:
She eases their fitting together
She is elbow room, lebensraum,
                    the vast spaces between the stars
She is eternally playful Lila: the universe is her toy
Alexa is goddess ex machina
She is the grace in the machine.

STAND UP FOR
DEE WISDOM WEED

Prohibition will work great injury to the cause of temperance. It is a species of intemperence within itself, for it goes beyond the bounds of reason in that it attempts to control a man's appetite by legislation and makes a crime out of things that are not crimes. A Prohibition Law strikes a blow at the very principles upon which our government was founded.

--Abraham Lincoln

On January 16, 1997, 38-year-old Will Foster, resident of Tulsa, Oklahoma, computer programmer, father of three children with no previous criminal record was fined $62,000 and sentenced to 93 years in prison for the crime of growing marijuana plants in his cellar. Foster claimed he smoked the herb because it relieved the pain of his rheumatoid arthritis.

Five hundred years ago, men tortured and killed innocent women for the crime of growing medicinal plants. In 21st-century America, armed agents of the state are forcibly entering private homes, separating hundreds of thousands of men and women from their families and imposing preposterous hardships upon them for the same offense.

Who are the real drug criminals--backyard herbalists like Will Foster or the men and women who have legalized Soviet-style atrocities in our own homeland?

DRUG NAZIS MUST DIE

MURDER IS MURDER under the sun
East or West robbers rob, rapists rape
But drink beer, wine, hashish
And out comes that leash
Who says who is caged, who shall run?
For drug crimes are made by the state, my son
Yes, drug crimes are made by the state.

A DRUG CRIMINAL sits in each lawmaker's seat
Crafting fictions to curb your desire
For medicine's balm, for love potion's charm
For doorway to God's holy fire.

Let's GET HARD ON DRUGS at the top of the chain
In the depths of each sinister lawmaker's brain
For each drug law they passes
We should CANE their bare asses
And castrate the ones who complain, mes amis
Yes, castrate the ones who complain.

FIRST PRESSING
AHLGREN VINEYARD 1998

Four tons of Chardonnay grapes
Trucked from Ventana in Big Sur
Dumped box by box
From truck bed into crusher
Slide down slippery wooden sluice
Into German-made wine press:
A ten-foot-long white-ribbed metal cylinder
Cast-iron hatches open, on its side
Like some beached research submarine
Out of the deep Pacific.

Elbow-deep in grape pulp and skins
We pack the steel press rim-full
Attach and latch four heavy iron doors
Jack up the crusher sluice
Back away the truck.

The whole press spins like a cement mixer
While black air-inflated rubber bladder inside
Squeezes out juices
Thru perforated stainless steel hull
Into drain trough below
Thick dripping essence--density-tested for sugar
Then sucked into wine pump
Pushed along intestine-resembling transparent
                                        plastic hose

Into thousand-gallon storage tank
Wedged behind Ahlgren's barrel-packed cellar
Where billion-year-old enzymes
Inside invisible one-celled minds
Pagan yeast, like Jesus at Cana
Turn water into wine.

Bodies sticky with juices
We assist in this miracle
Changing Big Sur air and sun
Into the taste of Chardonnay.

STOLEN DOPE
(for Craig)

Stand up for dee Wisdom Weed
Dee Rastaman's vote
Stay way from dee loser
Dat smoke stolen dope.

Stolen dope
Weaken dee muscle
Stolen dope
Make you tame

Stolen dope
Eat out dee brain stem
Stolen dope
Make you lame

Stolen dope
Make nobody like you
Stolen dope
Kill yer luck

Stolen dope
Dry up dee testicle
Stolen dope
Fuck you up

Stolen dope
Make you dumb, sick and ugly
Stolen dope
Turn off dee babes

Stolen dope
Help dee Man win his Drug War
Stolen dope
Give you AIDS.

Stand up for dee Wisdom Weed
Dee Rastaman's vote
Stay way from dee loser
Dat smoke stolen dope.

Dee mon dat grow dee Weed
Dat mon Hero
Dee mon dat steal dee Weed
Dat mon Thief

Dee mon dat steal dee Weed
Dee mon dat steal dee Weed
Dat mon, dat mon
Dat mon Thief.

JOYCE KILMER
THOU SHOULDST BE ALIVE
IN THIS HOUR

I think that I shall never see
(A-sittin' in my sauna)
A poem as lovely as, let's see
A grove of marijuana.

Her leaves reflect a lovely green
       Her blossoms give off spice
Her perfume draws the honeybee
       Methinks I dwell in paradise.

Writers, poets, music crews
       Use ganga as a door to Muse
And ardent lovers spread her fame
       For aid in Aphrodite's game.

Three thousand years her jagged leaves
       Have helped good doctors treat disease
And holy men from every sod
       Have praised her as a way to God.

Wise men from the Middle East
       Considered fine hashish divine
They taught that pot restrained the beast
       Beheaded fools who misused wine.

If I can sell baby-killing aspirin
Alcohol, rat poison, gasoline
Tobacco, dynamite and all the guns you need
Why can't I trade a single ounce of weed?

While stuffing pockets with our wealth
The politician schemes to stay in power
Screams: I can save you from yourself
By ordering low-paid cops to bust a flower.

Is pot really so bad for you and for me
That we hafta call out the bloody marines
Our back yards to assault, our assets to seize
In prisons to lock us for "growin' o' the green"?

I sing the spirit inside the seed
I praise the gorgeous Goddess weed
Poems are made by fools like me--and Dylan Thomas
But only God's the force
                   that thru the green fuse drives cannabis.

AYAHUASCA CIRCLE

Wearing human bodies
woven, so science says,
out of knotted yarns
called protein

This is what we do to seek vision
The desire not to look
The desire to fall asleep
is very strong.

This material
likes the dark.

It is strong
Let it flow thru you
Hum, moan, sing it
Give it voice.

I raise my hand
to greet you
soft and empty of blade
but my mind
is still a weapon.

Kiss the joy as it flies
Traps destroy the wingéd lives.

Jabir seeks the vitriol
that dissolves away matter
to reveal the pattern of lives and minds inside
to reveal the network of affection underneath
the strong invisible tendrils
upon which the universe
is draped like a blanket
across the shoulders
of a beautiful woman.

Would you like
a slice of ginger
to sweeten
the taste of it?

WORD-INTOXICATED SEEKERS OF THE REAL

ISLAM MEANS SUBMIT TO ALLAH
(A Moorish Orthodox Prostration
to Walt Bachrach)

Spaced-out bards
        and word-intoxicated seekers of the Real
we mine our lives
        we bare our hearts and heads, we grandly feel.
And we
Submit to Walt.

We worship sacred language,
        holy speech, enchanted sound
we praise the body,
        hog the podium, kiss the ground.
And we
Submit to Walt.

We leer, we wink,
        hike up our skirts, pull down our pants
we guzzle booze,
        we smoke, we venerate illegal plants.
And we
Submit to Walt.

We utter love songs,
        blessings, soft lullabies and curses
croon nursery rhymes,
        Gregorian chants and hot Satanic verses.
And we
Submit to Walt.

We worship Kenneth Patchen,
        Whitman, Rumi, Keats (or is it Kates?)
John Donne, e e cummings,
        William Blake and Butler Yeats.
And we
Submit to Walt.

We cultivate our darkness
        while we celebrate our light
Fall half in love with easeful death
        and rage against the Night.
And we
Submit to Walt.

Each Earthly thing is holy
Each second, Heaven--or a Hell
Each lady is a Goddess
Could we see beneath Her shell
Each man a living Buddha
And so we might as well
Submit to Walt.

HAPPINESS IN THE MOUTH

The Chinese characters for "Coca Cola"
spell "happiness in the mouth"
which we Americans find quaint
and a bit risque'

We say: all day my legs, my back,
                          my shoulders hurt
We never say: all night my knees, my neck,
                          my wrists were blissful

We all suffer head aches, tooth aches,
                          ear aches and belly aches
And how many heartaches have we felt? A lot.

But never are we gladdened by head joy, tooth joy,
                          ear joy or belly joy
And how often have we felt heart joy?
                          Not often enuf.

We are a nation of whiners!
Our language gives us away:

You make me sick
You hurt my feelings
You are a pain in the neck
You are a thorn in my side
You are a royal pain in the ass.

I say: get off my aching back!
Your constant bitching makes me sick!

You make me well
You gladden my feelings
You are a happiness in my throat,
                              a merriment in my bones
You are a delight in my pancreas
You are my blissful urethra
You are a royal joy in the ass

You are my body's felicity
You are my heart's delight
You are the bliss in my juices
You are a pleasure in every vertebrae
You are a happiness in the mouth.

THE ART OF PARTING

Even tho there are parts of the Earth
I never would have seen
Were it not for you

Even tho there are parts of the Music
I never would have heard
Were it not for you

Even tho there are parts of the Sea
I never would have smelled
Were it not for you

Even tho there are parts of me
I never would have tasted
Were it not for you

Even tho there are parts of you
I never would have touched...

Were it not for you

Were it not for you
I never would have learned

Were it not for you
I never would have learned
I can live without you.

DIE KUNST DER TRENNUNG

Es gibt einen Teil der Erde
Den Ich nie gesehen hätte
Wäre es nicht für Dich

Es gibt Musik
Die Ich nie gehört hätte
Wäre es nicht für Dich

Es gibt einen Teil des Meeres
Den Ich nie gerochen hätte
Wäre es nicht für Dich

Es gibt einen Teil von mir
Den Ich nie empfunden hätte
Wäre es nicht für Dich

Es gibt einen Teil von Dir
Den Ich nie berührt hätte...

Wäre es nicht für Dich

Wäre es nicht für Dich
Hätte Ich nie gelernt

Wäre es nicht für Dich
Hätte Ich nicht gelernt
Dass Ich ohne Dich leben kann.

trans. by Max Weiss

JABIR ON POLYGAMY

One woman
Is already
Too much.

PRIORITIES

Politics
Religion
Physics
Broadway hits

Nothing this moment so important
As the way
Light from the bedlamp
Illuminates your lips.

WHAT IS THE BODY?

The body is a sack of dung
says the Church: The body is a sin.
O no, says Science: The body is a machine;
The body is a sack of drugs.
The body means business, says the Company:
Each of the body's parts is a target
For aggressive Market Penetration;
The body is a sack of bucks.

I am all that and more, says the Body
I am a fiesta, I am a festival
I am a carnival of music, spirit, bones and goo
Now opening at six billion locations
Now opening at six billion locations near you.

The body is a sack of wonders
Now playing at six billion openings--
            at six billion openings near you.

O my lovely wide-spreadBody
      I am still examining
            still examining Your six billion openings.

VIRTUAL REALITY

Let's pretend to be perfect
Let's pretend to be bad
Let's pretend to be low life
Let's pretend to be mad

Let's rip off our clothing
And pretend to be holy
Let's dress up like cops
And go out patrolling

Let's pretend to be starving
Let's pretend we are fed
Let's pretend to be single
Let's pretend we are wed

Let's pretend to be prostitutes, porn stars
Medieval Russian saints
Let's pretend to be scientists, housewives
People with horrible complaints

Let's pretend we're telepathic
And read each other's minds
Let's pretend we're individuals
And live like porcupines

Let's pretend we are artists:
Ann Rice or Jimmy Joyce
Let's pretend to be what YOU want
Live in the daydream of YOUR choice

Pretend you're someone special
And I am special too
Prima donnas in a drama
Or fairy tale for two

With supporting cast of thousands
Playing enemies and friends
Who pretend to love and hate us
In ways we don't intend

Let's pretend we're evil devils
With stinky old cracks
Let's pretend we're good angels
With wings on our backs

Let's pretend we are gods
That run this whole show
And whatever we please
Is the way it will go

Let's play we are separate
Let's play we are One
Let's play we are dying
Pretending is fun

Let's pretend we are suffering
From a wound that won't heal
Let's forget we're pretending
Let's pretend it's all real.

KISS MY BARE ART

We drink our Muse; we smoke our Muse
We duct Her thru our gaping pores
Invent new sins to fan Her whims
We're lovely Muse's lowly whores.

We follow Muse beyond the stars
To bomb labs, muscle gyms and porno bars
Where Life beckons, there we go
Seek deeper meat than Jacques Cousteau.

We crave that rush, that punch, that flood
We love that dark orgasmic drain
Then pick ourselves up off the rug
And open up another vein.

For just one glance we drop our pants
Her prostitutes and renegades
Yet every kiss burns like the first
We're virginal as new-born babes.

THE WAY IT WORKS
(for Lulu)

O MotherWifeLoverChum

I pressed a nine-hundred-gauss
        refrigerator magnet against my balls
While thinking of you;
I blindfolded myself
        and sniffed your folded underclothing;
I learned French cooking,
        taichi chuan and celestial navigation
Just to impress you;
I awoke last night and kissed my mirror
Dreaming I was kissing you.

O MotherWifeLoverChum

If I have not been perseverant
In your service
It was because my enemy
Had distracted me.

O MotherWifeLoverChum

I think of you
Always.

NOT ADDICTION

Not addiction
Nor craving
The binding shall be light
As the choice of spice for breakfast
Like the Vine
Like the tendrils of the morning glory
In Zuleika's garden south of Tabriz:
Jabir recalls the hairs
Round Sophia's nipples.

NICHT SÜCHTIG

Weder Sucht
Noch Verlangen
Die Verbindung ist gering
Wie die Wahl der Würze fürs Früstück
Wie die Rebe
Wie die Ranke der Purpurwinde
Im Garten von Suleika im Süden von Taebris:
Jabir erinnert sich an die Haare,
Die Haare an Sophias Brust.

trans. by Max Weiss

MATH DANCE
(for Betsy)

Zeno and Parmenides both proved
that nothing in this world can move
Zoom!
Quick lady fox in leotard defeats
cracked logic of two armchair Greeks.

NEW LOVE
(for Fluffy)

My latest Lover is Mistress Death
A Lady I'm sure you all know
She'll tease you with maybes and almosts
But She never ever says No.

NO ANIMAL
(after Walt Whitman)

No animal badgers its mate.
No animal rats on its friends.
No animal sponges on its fellow man.

No animal joins that rat race
Crawling to its job
      in stinking metal box.

No animal works to outfox life
Worming every possible drop of joy
      from the lucky fact of sex.

No animal wolfs down drugs and high technology
To weasel its way out of the contract
Life long ago signed with Mister Death.

Without house insurance
Each animal raises young
In its nest.
Without car insurance
Each animal takes life
As it comes.
Without health insurance
Each animal faces death
Like a man.

PRAISE TO ICHTHOS

Ichthos, Ichthos, wet and salty
Ichthos, Ichthos, Queen of Fishes
Ichthos, Ichthos, Miracle Mollusk
Ichthos, Ichthos, grant my wishes

Praise Eve, the ancient Mother of us all
Praise Mary: Magdalene and Mother of Jesus
Praise Jezebel, Lilith, Sheba, Babylon's Holy Whore
Now worship glistening Ichthos on your kneeses

Praise the Holy Source of Nourishment
Honor Hathor, Egypt's Sacred Cow
Praise Her Milk, Her Breasts, Her Udders
And press your lips to sticky Ichthos now

Praise the Serpent in the Garden
Honor Golden Calf and Golden Bough
Worship Nature's every bump and aperture
And kiss the sacred slit of Ichthos now

Ichthos, Ichthos, wet and salty
Ichthos, Ichthos, Queen of Fishes
Ichthos, Ichthos, Miracle Mollusk
Ichthos, Ichthos, grant my wishes

Fear not
She's always cared for you (She always will)
Live strong and boldly in the Here and Now
Praise Pleasure, Life and every Trace of Goddess
Lick Ichthos please; lick Ichthos now
Lick Ichthos, yes lick Ichthos, lick Ichthos now
Lick Ichthos, yes lick Ichthos, lick Ichthos now.

MAMMOGRAM
(For Beverly before a breast exam)

To each creature who nurses
and bears its young alive

O bread-baking
tool-bearing
word-making
lipstick-wearing kin of
coyote, dolphin, leopard, ox
jaguar, weasel, whale, fox

May you be secure in your fur
In your flesh and its attachments
In the calcium and phosphorus
Of your bones

May you feed, sleep, breed
In season, as you please
Drinking deep of that sweet cup
Peculiar to your species

O star-gazer
trail-blazer
many-lovered
cotton-covered sister of
squirrel, oryx, ring-tailed cat
platypus, aardvark, vampire bat

May prey be abundant
Your teeth and muscles swift
Ears sharp, eyes clear
May your belly be full
Your blood hot and clairvoyant
May your mind be empty of fear

May every gash
         bite
         slash
         cut be healed
May your wounds make you wise

And when words finally fail you
All your powers falter
May you flee as Joyful Prey
Before the great Eater of All.

ODE TO ED
(for Ed Cramer)

An artist, a dreamer, a roustabout clown
a friend, a sativer, a man-about-town
a poet, a lover, a sly mischief-maker
a scholar, a shaman, a fine master baker
a lover of life and of yeast and of dough
and of things that go "squish" in the night.

You've seen the movie "Oklahoma"
It celebrates historic pride
where farmers, ranchers made their home--ah!
Well, Ed's folks were on the other side
and (if they could speak)
they'd sure want us to understand
we're squatting here tonight on Indian land.

What scent is that thru yonder window breaks?
Tis the smell of something good that bakes
Mayhaps some freaky pizza, magic muffins,
                                    grainful bread
We see, smell, touch and taste the genius of Ed
True Nature's hearty oven-tending fiend
he daily masterbakes behind the scenes.

In our Moorish Church, his holy name
is Grand Imam Omar abu Khan
Fakir of the Mountain's Teat
a friend to woman--and to "mon"

As part of his august profession
Omar's empowered to hear confession
Your guilt, your shame, your most obscene...
bring to Omar: he'll wipe you clean
With Omar, you never have to take a chance:
your sins are always pardoned in advance.

And Ed invented Captain Bathrobe
a champion in the war on drugs
who knows that downing tabs or mugs
of mind-perturbing chemistry
is part of ancient human history:
for where would we ignorant monkeys be
if you chopped off our curiosity?

To JJ's mountain lair he oft repaired
With Craig and Ashley, our lamented Buddhist bard
seduced by that hot flirtatious muse
of poetry to launch enormous argosies
of verse on love and death and life
and catch the scent of poet's paradise.

An artist, a dreamer, a roustabout clown
a friend, a sativer, a man-about-town
a poet, a lover, a sly mischief-maker
a scholar, a shaman, a fine master baker
a lover of life and of yeast and of dough
and of things that go "squish" in the night.

ELEMENTS OF TANTRA

Love every one of My Elements
Caress My Paradox
Embrace each phase-entangled photon
Hug My Molecules; kiss My Quarks.

The universe is My Body
From every eye, the glance is Mine
Down every river flow My Fluids
In every thing resides My Mind.

I loved you inside your mother's womb
Your every atom have I kissed
I've made you everything you are:
You treat Me like I don't exist.

When you open your eyes you gaze on My Body
You taste My Flesh with your lips
Every smell is My Sexual Attractant
Every touch is My Kiss.

Come open your sensors to Nature's flirtations
Come lend your step to My Dance
I'm only fourteen (billion) years old
But I'm eager and ripe for romance.

Love every one of My Elements
Caress My Paradox
Embrace each phase-entangled photon
Hug My Molecules; kiss My Quarks.